Alchemy of Ink and Blood

A Poetry Collection

Dana Hazem

First edition.
Published with love by The Quiet Rebellion Press.
Soft voices. Loud echoes.

ISBN (Paperback): 979-8-9989624-3-1

For my brother—
I've never been able to capture you in a poem,
but no one has shared more of this life with me.
In every memory, in every silence,
in every version of me—there you are.
This is for us, and the life we've lived side by side.

CONTENTS

SECTION I: Origins and Artifacts

Woven in Her Hands 2
What They Built 4
My First Doctor 5
Madar (Mother) 7
Roots and Orbits 9
Lefts and Rights 11
Your Voice, in Full Color 12
Reading the Air 14
Where the Rivers Learned to Run 16
The Great Ones 17
The Lamp 18
The Moon Wouldn't Tell Me 20
Elegy for Ease 23
Even Beauty Burns 24
The Bottle 25
Where It Ends 27

SECTION II: Descent and Disconnection

What I Carry 30
What I Cannot Carry 34
The Fabric That Knows 36
The Silent War 37
Ink and Water 39
The Silence We Inherit 40
Ringtone 42
Ich Komme (I'm Coming) 44
Misplaced in the Multiverse 46
The Quiet Trade 47
The Costs We Write Off 48
I Remember 49
After the Last Grasp 51
Built to Burn 52
Your Dream Girl 53

SECTION III: Attachment and Undoing

Holding Hope Alone 56
Where the Mouth Falters 57
A Quiet Undoing 58
Unfinished 59
Forms of the Blade 61
Never 63
Drafts 65
Conditional 67
Loving a Book by Its Cover 68
Lessons in Loving You 69
For Once 70
Read Receipts 71
Ode to the Idea of Him 73
Across the Room 75
The Quiet Break 77
The Art of Conditioning 79
Hollow Hunger 81
Four Counts 82
Finding Your Way Back to Yourself 84
The Earth Speaks 85
The Light at the Beginning 87

SECTION IV: Reclamation and Awakening

Again 89
The Girl I Owe 91
Reframing 93
Cosmic Law 95
Little Does She Know 96
No Logic in Love 97
Unmarked 98
The Path to Yourself 99
When the Roles Change 101
Fault Line 102
Who You've Always Been 103
The One Who Got Away 104

Confinement 106
Softness Up Close 107
The Sun Is My Lover 109
The Universe Inside Me 111
Where Love Goes 113
The Free Ones 114
Not Everything Green Will Grow 115
They Hold No Fire 116

SECTION V: Love and Becoming

The Ride of a Lifetime 118
The Quiet Rescue 120
Where Your Breath Lives 121
Ode to My Lover's Back 123
Topography 124
Two Weeks 126
Seasons of You 127
Exhibit 128
Sometimes 129
When the Wicks Align 131
Bahar (Spring) 132
What You Focus on Grows 133
Sanctuary 135
Boxing Classes 136
What Can't Be Bought 138
Maybe 139
Alchemy of Me 140
Be Productive 141
Quantum Creator 143
No Time 144
Where Silence Speaks 145
I Am Like the Sunset 146
The Universe Is Listening 148
For the One Who's Waiting 149

Oh, how grateful I am
to have moved mountains
to be here.

SECTION I

Origins and Artifacts

The roots I stand on, still lifting, still anchoring me.

Woven in Her Hands

The pursuit of happiness
was clenched in my mother's left hand—
a single thread unwinding
through her mother's headscarf,
from the moment she was born
in the province of Herat,
western Afghanistan.

As war rained on her home,
and family portraits faded,
she gripped the thread tighter.
Her mind—
her heart—
only expanded.

She pulled us along that thread,
crossing border after border,
beneath skies
sewn with stars
we could not recognize.

Surviving.
Still in pursuit.

Thread in one hand,
family in the other—
sacrifice after sacrifice,
building homes
only to leave them behind.

Homes with orchards,
where fruit hung heavy
native only to the trees
outside her window in Herat—
fruit she would never taste again.

But she wove that thread into shelter.
She wrapped it around us.
She wove a life—
sewed the clothes on my back,
bound my schoolbooks with it,
stitched my medical school emblem
onto my white coat.

And then,
with a steady hand,
she passed me the remainder of the thread—
the toughest strand known to man—
and said:

Build your life—let it mirror the vastness within you.

And as I made my way
across the country,
I left pieces of it behind,
tied like trail markers
so I'd always find
my way back home.

What They Built

My parents arrived on American soil
with seven hundred dollars
and two kids
held tightly between them.

They crossed borders
with nothing but will and wonder,
and built a temple—
not of stone,
but of hope.

They planted diamonds in our minds
that spoke of perseverance,
flowers in our hearts
that whispered kindness.
They handed us tools
crafted from empathy and compassion,
kept our bellies full,
our minds wide open.

They built a castle
of golden dreams
and sapphire thoughts.
They painted the walls
with poetry,
with philosophy,
with stories passed down
like sacred cloth.

Then, they climbed the tallest summit,
attached wings to our backs,
and let us soar.

My First Doctor

My grandmother was a doctor—
but not in the way you might think.

She tended to the sick
with hands that steadied more than bodies,
with eyes that saw beyond the surface,
and a voice that calmed storms
before they began.

She cleaned out wounds
found not only on skin,
but in minds.
She never reached for ethanol or gauze—
only presence,
only love.

She repaired damaged hearts
without ever lifting a scalpel.
She saw the soul
standing before her
and healed the parts
no chart would capture.

My grandmother worked long days,
and longer nights—
carrying a kind of strength
that did not announce itself.

She didn't flinch at chaos.
She walked straight through it.
Even when she was tired,
she showed up whole.

Her mind was astute,
her instincts unerring—
but it was her heart,
the way it made space for everyone,
that taught me the most.

She was caring and kind.
Resilient.
Selfless.
Wise.

No white coat.
No initials after her name.
Just a life poured into others.

They'll call me "Doctor" one day.
I'll earn the title,
carry the degrees.

But *Dada Jaan*—
she is the one
who practiced greatness
in silence,
without applause,
long before I ever picked up a stethoscope.

My grandmother was the doctor
I aspire to be.

Madar *(Mother)*

The story of your life
is far too heavy
for the spine of any book,
or the bones of any one person to carry.

Chapters carved from silence and sacrifice,
from dreams tucked into dresser drawers,
from love spoken not in words,
but in the way you filled empty rooms
with safety.

Yet you walk—
gracefully,
as if your sorrow were not a weight,
but a rhythm.

You love—
tenderly,
as if pain had only softened you
into something more human,
more whole.

You are light—
not because life spared you,
but because you chose—
again and again—
to rise,
to give,
to shine.

The world may never hold your full story,
but I carry pieces of it
in the way I speak,
in the way I care,
in the way I learn to love—
like you.

Roots and Orbits

My father is my astronomy teacher—
he shows me the stars, one by one,
naming constellations
as if they were old friends.

My father is my naturalist—
we walk through woods
as he teaches me the language
of leaves, rivers, and wind.

My father is my science guide—
he tells stories of atoms and galaxies,
of curious minds
and daring discoveries.

My father is my English professor—
he reads me poems under lamplight,
his voice unfolding
worlds made of words.

My father is my music mentor—
he filled our home with melodies,
and let me find my own rhythm
in their echo.

My father is my historian—
he tells me of empires, rebels, and thinkers,
of the world
before I knew it.

He teaches me
nature,
adventure,
love,
pain—
and how to walk through it all.

Lefts and Rights

At age 1:
Right, left—
right, left.
My mother guided me
as she taught me
how to walk.

At age 12:
"Defender on your left!"
"She's open on your right!"
My parents shouted
from the sidelines
at my basketball games.

At age 16:
Right, then left—
then right, left here.
My father directed me
as he taught me
how to drive.

At age 18:
Right, then the first left,
now the second right,
and then on the left—
I steered my parents
to my college dorm room.

At age 21:
I make all the lefts,
and take all the right turns,
to find my way back home.

Your Voice, in Full Color

I used to be embarrassed
by the way you spoke—
it was always so different
from everyone else.

I used to correct and scold you.
I was always so harsh.

I picked at your German pronunciations
and Dari translations—
depriving you of every color
that beamed off your skin,
stripping away your magic,
shrinking you down
to fit in a box.

How dare I attempt
to destroy such beautiful art?

I used to wish you blended in—
until I realized
the brilliance in standing out.

I now cherish your every word.

My ears long to be awakened
by your voice and all its flavors—
your accent,
carrying stories through generations;
your dialect,
tracing deep into the seeds you planted,
creating a life for yourself

time and again.

The sweetest sap comes from the strongest
roots—
and every flower you grew is proof.

I now stand proud
by the way you speak—
it is always so different
from everyone else.

Reading the Air

You were raised
to pick up on the cues—
the little nuances
no one else seemed to catch.

The lift of an eyebrow,
the faint crease of a forehead.
The sigh—
not from the lips,
but from the eyes.

A single-decibel
shift in someone's voice.
A slowness in their blink—
not tired,
but heavy
with something unspoken.

You noticed
when their tone
held too much air,
when their words
landed in the wrong octave,
when their shoulders
slouched in ways
they didn't yesterday.

You learned
to scan the room like radar,
to map emotion
from silence.

To track storms
before anyone else
could smell the rain.

You were praised
for being intuitive.
But really—
you just had to pay attention.
Because safety
often depended
on what went unsaid.

Where the Rivers Learned to Run

Mother Nature wears a thousand faces—
storms and petals, frost and fire.
She is the hush of snowfall,
the slow promise of spring,
the endless voice of the sea.

And amidst the wild, I find myself most at home.
Maybe it's because I've seen it before:
the earth, aching to imitate
my mother's divine ability
to summon gardens
where there was once only stone.

The rivers only learned to run
because my mother's voice taught them—
soft, steady, unafraid to carve through stone.
The trees lean toward light
the way I leaned toward her,
rooted by her hands,
rising toward her open sky.

The seasons change; my mother never does.
Still blooming, still burning,
still the blueprint of every good thing
the world ever tried to emulate.

So let them praise the mountains and tides,
let them write poems for the forests—
I will sing of my mother:
the root beneath every forest,
the loving whisper in the wind,
the name the rivers still carry home.

The Great Ones

Greatness
doesn't arrive with applause.
It grows inward—
silently,
like roots beneath the soil.

It isn't made of titles,
or the weight of what you own—
but by how gently you hold
what isn't yours.
By how truthfully
you live
when no one's watching.

The ones who walk
with honesty—
even when the path is lonely,
even when no one cheers—
they are the ones
who stand tall
at the end of the way.

The Lamp

I moved the last of your stuff out yesterday.
But I'm still standing here,
staring at the final piece of furniture left.

I can't bring myself to get rid of it.

The lamp.

The same lamp that stood tall
on your side of the bed,
casting light over the quiet parts of you.

The lamp we knocked over
one night—
laughing, tangled,
too carried away to care.

The lamp
I once wanted to smash
just to hear the sound
of something shattering
that wasn't us.

It's seen it all—
our glory,
our unraveling.

If it could talk,
it would tell stories we never shared,
give away our secrets
to the whole town.

I remember the day we bought it—
how we picked it out,
set it gently beside us.
As if it might light the way
to somewhere we didn't know how to go.

Today,
I took it to the flea market
and left it behind.

I watched a couple
discover it excitedly,
hands brushing
as they carried it off.

I wondered
when they'll realize—
the bulb's burned out.

The Moon Wouldn't Tell Me

Every night,
I find myself staring at the sky,
looking deep into the moon's eyes.

I don't know how I came to believe
that it knows your secrets—
but I do.

So every night,
I gaze at it, hoping it'll reveal something.
Where you went.
How you are.
If you can feel me.

But the moon never says a thing.

So I trace its lines with my eyes,
thinking maybe they'll lead me your way.
I analyze its face,
hoping it'll tell me you're okay.

I beg it to speak.
But it just looks back at me.
Still.
Silent.
Glowing, like it knows more than it lets on.

I take the notebook
in which you taught me to write,
and I log its changing face, dusk after dusk—
searching for patterns,
searching for answers.

I come back every night.
I talk to it for hours.
Sometimes we argue.
Sometimes we cry together.
Sometimes we ponder life
and its meaning.

But when I ask about you—
it goes quiet.
It just stares,
with a look I still don't understand.
Not cruel,
not kind.
Just… knowing.

Yet when the sun sets,
I return.
And after endless nights of pleading,
after months of silence,
enough time has passed
for me to learn:

The only answer
is that there isn't one.

So, beloved grandfather,
Hajji Baba Jaan—

I speak to you in my thoughts,
and in my dreams.
I carry you in my breath,
and in my laugh.
I hold you in my heart,
and in my poems.

I see you
in the trees
and in the birds
that soar over me.
I hear you
in songs
and in the howling of the wind.

I feel you
when the air fills my lungs.
I feel you
in the arms of my mother.

And I know—
the moon wouldn't tell me.

But I know—
you can feel me too.

Elegy for Ease

I don't want to be resilient anymore.
I want ease.
I want comfort.

I don't want to be looked at in awe,
praised for what I had to overcome.
I want simplicity.

I don't want to be known
for my strength and courage.
Be gentle with me.

I don't want to know all the answers anymore.
I want permission to be lost—
to look to someone else for guidance.
Protect me.

I don't want the adversity I face to be unique.
I want to be mundane—
ignorantly happy.

I no longer want to set forests ablaze
to create my own path.
I want to walk on polished pavement,
intentionally laid down for me.

I want resilience to be a choice,
for when I'm feeling up for a challenge—
not my only option,
as it has always been.

Even Beauty Burns

It's like I'm cursed.

Pain hurts.
Sorrow hurts.

But also—
love hurts.
Happiness hurts.
Inspiration hurts.
Family hurts.

I ache from the lack of love,
then I ache from its abundance.

I cry for the hurt others cause,
then I cry for the hurt I cause in return.

I grieve when I'm being yelled at,
then I grieve
when I yell back.

Even stillness aches.
Even beauty burns.

It's like I was made
with no skin—
just nerve endings.

To feel everything
is a gift.

And a sentence.

The Bottle

I first saw it when I was two.
I didn't know what it meant—
just glass and absence.

At four, I shrank when the bottle spoke.

At six, I watched it steal you away.
You looked like my dad,
but you didn't sound like him.
You didn't *feel* like him.

At eight, I saw it and froze—
fear baked into my bones.

At ten, I stopped knowing
where the nightmare ended.

At twelve, I begged you to quit—
so often
my knees bled.

At fourteen,
I learned how to vanish without leaving.

At sixteen,
I kept giving you chances
because I didn't know
I didn't have to.

At eighteen,
I went months without speaking to you.
Silence became safer than hope.

At twenty,
I mistook numbness for healing.

Now,
at twenty-two,
I look at it
and see lifetimes of pain.

I see anger.
I see sorrow.
I see a child
who never stopped loving you—
but finally stopped chasing you.

I see myself.

And I ask,
with bloodshot eyes
and a heart heavy as stone:

*How could you love the bottle
more than you love me?*

Where It Ends

A witness to pain.
A testament to life—
strained,
same blueprints,
same shadows,
etched into each day.

A curse I didn't choose,
only inherited—
passed down like breath,
like blood.
Handed to me
before I ever set foot
on this earth.

Lifetimes lived
fighting for you—
because you were all I knew.
Gripping the edges of survival,
calling it love,
calling it life.

Or so I thought.
A misconstrued set of instructions,
copied and carried
until they became
my truth.

All I know is you.
All I know is anger,
pain,
grief,

struggle.

But soon—
I will have *known* you.
And I will set you down
like old armor.

Because what I will know,
what I will choose,
what I will live—
will be greater
than the story I was given.

SECTION II

Descent and Disconnection

When the cracks deepen, and everything breaks.

What I Carry

My breath gets shallow as I brace myself.
You open your mouth to speak—
and the moment I hear your voice,
my heart starts racing.

I've been here
far too many times.

I look into your eyes,
but you're long gone.
Fright settles
into the contours of my heart—
and I know it's going to stay awhile.

With shaking hands,
I grab onto you.
I try to hold you up
as your body leans
entirely into mine.

This was harder
when I was a kid.

I struggle
to walk you to the car.
I know what comes next—
a balancing act:
drive smoothly,
minimize the bumps,
keep the window cracked for air.

I hold my breath
the whole way home,
bracing
for what I expect.

You vomit on yourself.
I try to suppress my senses.
I count down the miles
like prayers
until we're back in the driveway.

Then comes the waiting game—
how long until you agree
to go inside?

An hour passes.
You finally cooperate.
I carry you in,
catching you as you fall.

Onto the couch.
Essentials:
water, blankets, towels.

Once you fall asleep,
I allow myself to cry.
It goes on
until my head aches
enough to make me stop.

I sit near you,
awake through the night,
afraid of the damage
you've done

to your body.
I check your breathing.
I move the towel from your mouth
so you won't choke.

It's 3 a.m. now,
and I finally let myself wonder:

What are you trying to forget?
What fire burns in you
so violently
you have to drown it?

How can I help you?
What can I do?

You won't talk about it—
not to me,
not to anyone.
It's too big,
even for your own mind
to hold.

An hour later,
you wake abruptly
and vomit again.
I shut my eyes and ears.
I'm still not used to the sound.

You sleep again.
I keep watch.
Make sure you're still breathing.

By dawn,
my panic starts to settle.
I look at your face—
so peaceful,
so innocent.

I see the little boy
who saw more than a child ever should—
the one who needed love and safety
but was handed storms, not shelter.

And I ache
from the pain you put me through.
But I burn
from the pain
I see inside of you.

So, I whisper:
"I don't blame you."

Because how can I be angry
at a victim?

What I Cannot Carry

Here we are—
yet another night,
your body swaying,
too heavy for mine,
my tiny arms trying
to hold you upright
like a child catching
a falling tree.

I guide us home
through silence and stumbles,
and ask you, softly,
Why?

Why do you drink
until your voice disappears?
Until your eyes glaze over
like they've traveled somewhere
I cannot follow?

You look at me
and say,
"Dele man ba suz ast." (*My heart burns with sorrow.*)

Five words.
That's all.
But they land
like shattered glass
in my chest.

I didn't know
a sentence could
undo me.

My anger fades
into something worse—
understanding.
A quiet grief
that's not mine,
yet suddenly is.

What are you trying
to drown
that I'm not allowed to see?

Why won't you let me
carry the story,
instead of just
the weight?

Now your pain
sits beside mine,
heavier still.
Piling on
like rain
on soaked clothes—
a sorrow too wet to wring out.

And yet, still not enough to keep me from
burning.

The Fabric That Knows

I need to do laundry.
I have no clean pillowcases—
when I rest my head at night,
they catch what I can no longer hold.

After a long day of battle,
my body no longer listens.
So my pillowcases carry the weight
of everything I cannot say aloud.

I am ready to accept defeat.
There's nothing left in me—
I've exhausted every option,
burned through every prayer.

I've already been torn apart.
What difference does it make
if I sever a tie
that might finish the job?

You've drained
my mind, my body, my soul.
So I lay my head
on a damp, salty pillowcase
and let it take what's left.

The Silent War

A silent and dreadful stillness—
a crime of perpetual damage
without a single witness.

It slithers into my head,
unraveling my brain,
poisoning my thoughts along the way.

It rips, tears, splits me apart
until there is nothing left
but a war-torn city,
My Mind, Population: 1.

I am both victim and perpetrator,
serving a life sentence
within myself.

My body aches
as every bone shatters inside me,
every muscle tears,
every organ shuts down.

I can't escape the war—
it lives in me.
I can't calm the storm—
I'm the fuel.
I can't stop the pain—
it's carved into my being,
woven through the fabric
of my existence.

My world is in combat,
but no one hears a sound.
My mind and body
have gone mad—
but no aid can be sent.
All connections to the outside world: severed.

These moments
have no time limit,
no cure,
no warning
of when they'll occur once more.

The shadow wanders—
but never leaves.
As if it, too,
is imprisoned with no escape.

It's made itself at home,
against all wishes—
infiltrating my body,
settling in the ridges.

Ink and Water

As pen touches paper,
staining its fibers,
I feel an instant sense of ease.

As ink carves into the page,
the clouds begin to clear,
the fog begins to fade,
the pressure begins to lift.

I have brought my demons into the light—
and now, I can begin to defeat them.

My mind bathes
in a pool of thoughts.
Inside my head,
the water stirs gently.

I feel relaxed.
In control.

I acknowledge the flow—
a current pressing
against the dam in my mind.

Then I let it pour.

And as the tension drains away,
I realize:
we must breathe
until the ripples soften,
until the water welcomes us in,
and we find our way back to ourselves.

The Silence We Inherit

This stillness—
is one found
in too many of my people.

For the heart can only take so much.
The stomach,
can only be empty for so long.
The lungs—
they can only fight against pressure
for a brief moment
before surrendering.

An unfathomable pain,
overcome
by exhaustion.
Until nothing remains
but stillness.

In times of extreme trauma to the body,
the spinal cord blocks pain signals
from reaching the brain.

But when the trauma is
to the brain itself—
what then?

How will it tell the heart
to keep beating?
The blood
to keep flowing?

What incentive does it have
to keep the lungs
reaching for breath?

How does it carry on,
raw and ruptured,
without protection,
without a defense line?

Open.
Vulnerable.
Bracing for defeat.

Ringtone

I called you today.
The phone was ringing.

It felt like I was calling customer service—
not knowing who'd be on the other line,
what their name was,
if it would be a pleasant experience
or an unpleasant one.

My heart racing.
You answer.

I use the noises in the background
as context clues—
trying to guess where you are,
how you're doing.
That's the only way
I get any information about you
nowadays.

As I speak to you,
each word trembles out of me,
as if tripping over my teeth
on its way out.

It takes my entire being
to mask agony as indifference—
to build a dam behind my eyes,
to hold back the tears
urged out
every time the sound of your voice
lands on my ears.

My senses were never good at cooperating.

Who would've thought
we'd end up here?

If anyone had overheard our conversation,
they'd never guess
we were once
father and daughter.

But here we are.

And life goes on, right?
At least that's what they keep telling me.

But life doesn't go on—
not the life I knew.
Not the life I embraced.

I find myself stuck.
Stuck on every word uttered
in the last twenty-three years.
Adhered to the pain—
your pain.

Clinging to your traces.
Examining the stains in the carpet,
the residue on your clothes
left behind,
hanging intact
in the bedroom closet—
with no body
to fill them.

Ich Komme *(I'm Coming)*

Lately,
the days have been long and tired,
and the nights settle in colder than before.
Goosebumps rise like tiny prayers,
reaching up,
hoping for your touch.

You were the only one
who ever knew how to calm them—
the only one who made the ache feel less loud.

This is the longest
I've gone without your voice.
And I'm scared—
scared I might forget the sound,
or the way it wrapped around my anxiety
like a blanket that never asked questions.

I never could've imagined
it would hurt this much.

I'm past the anger,
past the arguing,
past the keeping score.
At the end of the day—
I just miss you.

I miss hearing your voice.
I miss your hugs.
Looking into your honey eyes
and knowing you saw me—

truly saw me—
for all that I am.
Wholeheartedly loved me.

And in the quiet,
when the ache grows too wide for my chest,
I still hear the child in me—
shouting as she runs down the stairs,
shoes barely on her four-year-old feet:
Baba, Ich komme!
Baba, Ich komme!

Misplaced in the Multiverse

This pain is different.
It's the kind that deems life unworthy.
It is not meant for any human to bear.

There must have been a tear
in the fabric of the cosmos,
causing it to fall onto my chest—
a weight only species from other galaxies
might have the capacity to carry.

This pain may allow life to continue
in another universe,
but not in this one.

My human lungs are far too fragile.
It wraps around each of them and clenches;
they do not have the strength to keep expanding.
My breath grows shallow—
until it eventually stops.

This pain is not meant for our world.
My heart was not designed to endure it.
It squeezes my four chambers
until I'm void of every drop of blood.
My heartbeat slows—
until it eventually stops.

I can't make sense of this pain.
But I know—
like the human body—
it must, eventually,
stop.

The Quiet Trade

Why have I always been
so good at holding pain
that wasn't mine?

Simple—other people's sorrow
was easier to lift.
It came in shapes I could carry:
a wilted flower,
a cracked glass,
a song I didn't write
but knew how to hum.

My own pain?
It was a room with no door.
A sky pressed to my chest.
Weightless,
yet suffocating.
Unseen,
yet always there.

So I became a vessel
for other people's ache—
a shelf,
a lantern,
a pair of arms
built for catching
what was never thrown to me.

Because carrying yours
meant I never had to sit alone
with the heavy silence
of my own.

The Costs We Write Off

Temporary pleasure
always comes back
in the form
of a permanent scar.

It arrives soft,
sweet,
easy—
a warmth in the dark,
a hand to hold
when you're slipping.

But it never stays.

It leaves behind
what it never promised—
bruises
you learn to call your own,
silences
you can't explain,
a version of yourself
you barely recognize.

Temporary pleasure
always leads
to permanent damage.

And yet,
sometimes,
we chase it anyway—
hoping this time,
it won't hurt as much.

I Remember

I know you'll never admit it.
But I notice.

I see the way you look at me now—
and I remember
the way you used to look at me then.
Starved for my presence.

In love with me—
with everything I did,
everything I was.
You were delighted
just to see me.
To be near me.

I lived that love
through my own eyes,
until something shifted.

Now—
your body doesn't reach for mine
like it used to.
Your hands don't find me
without thought.

You don't jump
at the chance to hold me.

Each kiss feels like a task.
Each hug, a checked box.
Each embrace, a formality.

And I still remember
the world from her eyes—
and what it felt like
to be reached for
like breathing—
natural,
instinctive,
undeniable.

Now I'm just air
you've learned to live without.

After the Last Grasp

It's like we're all
peacefully letting go.

No resistance.
No protest.
Just silence,
and slow release.

I open my grasp
and let myself fall.

Not out of hope,
but because
I have no energy left
to hold on—
not to this life,
not to you.

How do we stop
the pain?
The hurt?

I don't know.
I only know
I'm tired.

And sometimes,
peace
looks like surrender.

Built to Burn

You had us build this place—
with bare hands and shared hopes,
brick by brick,
vow by vow.

You asked me to stay.
You said this was home—
that *we* were home.

Then one day,
you lit a match—
sparked a flame
just to see what would burn.

And before the smoke had time to rise,
you were already
gone.

Leaving me
in the house we built—
walls collapsing,
heat at my heels,
calling it love
as you walked away
into the air you never let me breathe.

Your Dream Girl

She's your perfect type—
the one you used to describe
when we whispered our dreams aloud.

Her hair?
That sunlit shade
that always caught your eye.

Her body?
Like you sculpted it yourself—
the way she moves
through the world like it belongs to her.

If you got to know her,
you'd find out
her dream city is yours.
She runs your favorite trails at dawn.
She knows your teams—
they're hers too.

She's the kind of girl
you'd spot in a crowd and know,
without question:
she's the one.

And if you met her,
the rest would be history.

But you didn't.
You met me.

And now I get to see her—

every day.
Up close.
From afar.
In the reflection of everything
I thought I had to become
to make you stay.

SECTION III

Attachment and Undoing

What I didn't know I was losing.

Holding Hope Alone

I wish it had been us.
I wish I'd known the parts of you
that felt unlovable—
I would have wrapped them gently in my hands,
loved them a little louder,
a little longer.

I wish you'd known
the ways I needed safety—
not from the world,
but from the quiet unraveling
that begins
when I'm left holding hope alone.

I pictured us in softer light,
in rooms where no one left,
in futures where love was easy,
and staying
was just the natural thing to do.

I still dream of the version
where it was you—
where all our almosts became always,
and silence
was filled with the sound of us.

But it wasn't.
Maybe it couldn't be.
Still—
sometimes, I find myself
wishing it were.

Where the Mouth Falters

What do you say
to the only one
who's ever made you feel alive?

The only one
who's truly seen you—
not just your face,
but the corners of your soul
you keep in shadow.

What do you say
to the soul
who lights a fire in you,
just to keep you warm?

You ask me why I stutter—
why I trip over my own thoughts,
repeating
"like"
and *"um"*
and
"like"
and
"um,"
like I'm trying to stall the inevitable.

But tell me—
what do you say
when every cell in your body
is screaming *love*,
and your mouth
just can't catch up?

A Quiet Undoing

Does it count as love—
if I see your heart
and you see mine?

Does it count as self-punishment—
if I imagine our future
knowing it will never come to fruition?

Does it count as ignorance—
if I allow myself to keep falling
knowing you're incapable
of catching me?

Does it count as injustice—
if you're all I've ever wanted,
but there are oceans between us?

Does it count as a loss—
if I've only ever held you
in my mind?

Does it count as heartbreak—
if I'm breaking my own heart,
chipping off pieces,
and placing them
in your hands?

Does it count as grief—
if I know there will come a time
when I live each day
longing for your soul,
missing you?

Unfinished

I keep the idea of you—
perfectly preserved—
tucked into the back pocket
of the jeans I wore
the day you walked away.

Because somehow,
I find solace in the void.
Comfort in the gaping hole
you left behind.

I've built a home there,
in the ache.
It's given me shelter,
a quiet corner to stay warm.

I'm sorry
if I left you broken—
torn in two directions.

But I had to let go
of the rope that tied me
to the left side of your body—
the one ruled
by the right side of your brain.

The artist in you.
The wild in you.
The one who painted with chaos
and loved me
without logic.

I had to let go—
before I became
a canvas
you forgot to finish.

Forms of the Blade

How much longer can we go
breaking our hearts
a little more
each day?

This—
this is the true torture:
staring love in the face,
knowing
it will never be
our fate.

Admiring from worlds apart.
Embracing
with barricades between us.
Holding one another—
but only
in the words we etch
on paper.

We can no longer go on
tearing ourselves apart
with the pens we use
to declare our love—

or the blades
we use to carve it
into sentences,
into stanzas,
into scars.

Love should not feel
like writing
on open wounds.

And yet—
here we are,
bleeding beauty
just to feel
close.

Never

For you,
I'd give it all—
my skin,
my bones.

I'd carve a piece of flesh
from around my stomach,
cut it out clean
just to prove
you mattered more.

I'd give you
my energy,
my thoughts,
my time—
so you'd always have
more than enough.

For you,
I'd pick your team,
cheer from the sidelines,
even if you never looked back.

I'd offer you
every first and last bite
of my favorite food.

For you,
I would cry an ocean
just to give you distance,
space enough
to breathe.

For you,
I'd bite my tongue
to keep our conversations
from diving deeper
than you could bear.

I'd slouch—
lower my head,
let my crown fall—
so yours could shine
a little brighter,
sit a little taller.

For you,
I'd lose every game
without a fight,
just to watch you win.

For you,
I gave it all—
my flesh,
my bones.
And now,
there's nothing left
of me
that wasn't for you.

Drafts

If I leave,
please know—
it was not because I stopped loving you.

It was because my heart
grew too weak.
The pain became too much.

When love has nowhere to go,
it turns inward—
folding in on itself
until it starts to bruise the body
that holds it.

I had to go
before it exploded.
Before I shattered
under the weight
of what I could not say.

If I leave,
please know—
it was because I loved you
more than I was supposed to.

If I leave,
please know—
my chest could no longer carry
the heaviness
of unspoken love.

If I leave,
please know—
I still hope
you find yourself
in my absence.

Clarity in the silence.
Peace in the space.
And love,
even in the place
where I no longer am.

Conditional

His love has terms.
Conditions.
Like when I'm at my best—
happy and lifting him up,
standing tall beside him,
smiling on cue.

Not when I'm tired,
in need of support—
someone to help
carry some of the weight.

He loves me
when I make him feel strong—
not when I need strength myself.

I wonder
how he could watch me
curl inward with disappointment—
and do nothing.

But I can't make him see.
And that might be
the loneliest part of all.

Loving a Book by Its Cover

You told me to show you
how much I loved you.

So, I wrote it out.
I used every fiber of my heart
as the pencil,
every ounce of my blood
as the ink.

I tore myself apart,
thread by thread,
and poured my entire being
into a three-volume set
of poetry books.

I wrote and wrote and wrote
until I bled out.
I gave and gave and gave
until there was nothing left of me.

But the books were finally done.
And you would finally see
my love for you.

Turns out—
you love books
with pretty covers,
but you hate
to read poetry.

Lessons in Loving You

I can't make you care.
I can't place your hands on my hips
and show you how to pull me in.

I can't script your mouth
to say the right words
when I'm falling apart.

I can't make you notice
the small things—
the ones that mean everything.

I can't teach you
the language of my energy.

And by being with you,
I'm losing myself.
I watch my confidence wither,
my voice grow quiet,
my light dim—
until it disappears.

I must unlearn
what you taught me
without words.

Return to myself—
to gather the pieces
you didn't see,
and love them
like I always hoped
you would.

For Once

I wanted you
to fight for me.
To not give up
so easily.

For once,
I wanted someone
to tell me what I needed.
To show me—
so my mind could finally fall silent.

I wanted someone
I could depend on,
after only ever
knowing independence.

To release the tension
in my mind.
To surrender my body
into yours.
To let my lungs cave in—
and somehow still be sustained.

To finally give in
to the exhaustion
of being on my own.

I guess,
for once,
I wanted to be told
that I don't always
know what's best for me.

Read Receipts

Let's play a game.
Let's guess how many times
I pick up and put down my phone,
yearning for a message from you.

Waiting.
Refreshing.
Reaching for a reply
that never comes.

Each time I check,
all I see
is my own reflection
on a dark screen—
eyes full of hope,
now dimmed
by silence.

And it's in that silence
that doubt finds room.
It creeps in,
one small worry
becoming a hundred more.

I try to fill the emptiness—
but nothing quite fits
the space where you should be.

So I lay the phone down
one more time,
try to shake off
the ache.

But disappointment sets in
like a shadow that lingers.

And now I'm left
with echoes and feelings
I thought I'd outgrown.

Ode to the Idea of Him

I never loved *him*—
not truly.
I loved the version I imagined
in the quiet between his words.
I loved the shadow he cast
when the light was mine.

He didn't make things magical—
I did.
It was my laughter echoing in the room,
my stories filling the silence,
my joy spilling into every moment
and making it feel like something
worth remembering.

I mistook his stillness for presence,
his detachment for depth.
I filled the gaps in his affection
with my own tenderness
and called it connection.

I thought he made me feel alive.
But it was my spark
reflected in his glassy eyes.
I brought the color.
I set the tempo.
I made it worth staying for.

And now I see it clearly—
it wasn't him I was drawn to.

It was *me*,
mirrored faintly
in the idea of him.

What I loved
was my own light
dancing
in someone else's shadow.

Across the Room

You,
so full of color—
settling for gray.

You,
so open-hearted—
trapped behind walls you didn't build.

So how does that work?

Hands that would hold you gently,
eyes that would see you clearly,
hearts that would rise like tides for you—
still,
you stay where love forgets your name.

So how does that work?

You brush off the bruises you don't show,
you excuse the silence you don't deserve.
You wear sorrow like a second skin,
and call it home.

So how does that work?

If I could—
I would build you a new language,
one where love never sounds like fear.

A thousand protests catch fire inside,
burning the words I'll never say.

But what can I do?

I'm left loving you—
quietly, deeply—
from across the room.

Because that's just how it works.

The Quiet Break

I wear a smile—
a disguise I crafted
to keep the hurt hidden,
to mask the hollow echo
beneath my ribs.

I reach for you,
try to hold your hand—
but your fingers
are wrapped in thoughts
of anything
but us.

I ache
for closeness,
for something real—
a tether,
a deeper bond.

But the space between us
grows wider
with every silent night.

The distance in miles
means nothing
compared to the mountains
we refuse to climb.

Separation
by sedimentation—
layers of what we left unsaid,
packed down by time and silence.

We've become
a fault line—
still connected,
but under pressure,
waiting for the quiet break.

The Art of Conditioning

I could train myself to love.
My heart might not flutter
when you walk in the room,
but I could train it
to race.

My eyes may not light up
when they see you,
but I could teach them
to stay fixed.

My mind may not be
flooded with thoughts of you,
but I could retrace our steps,
rerun our days
until memory became desire.

You didn't want me
to give up on us—
so I didn't.

Mind over matter,
my coaches used to say.
And I knew how to do this.
So I trained.

I ran across every terrain.
I arranged my feelings
like furniture.
But how strange.
How strange it all became.

I learned to confuse aggression
with passion.
To interpret crossed boundaries
as closeness.
To call my fear excitement
my discomfort novelty.

I didn't notice—
until it was too late—
that all my skies
were painted gray,
and I had trained myself
into someone
I didn't want to be.

Hollow Hunger

You are still unkind—
still hollow in ways
no one else can fill.

You move toward bodies
as if warmth
could replace meaning,
as if desire
might teach you
how to feel.

Love had already come to you—
in open palms and patient eyes.
But you turned from it.
You didn't yet know
how to stay soft
long enough to receive it.

Now, you chase
what vanishes by dawn.
You run after sparks
and call them fire,
never waiting
to feel the heat.

Love has gone quiet in your hands.
And still,
you call it elusive—
never admitting
you let it slip
before you learned
how to hold it.

Four Counts

If you were the one,
tell me.
Blink twice,
send smoke signals three thousand miles.
Hurry—
before I drift further away.

If you were the one,
put a bounty on my head.
Send two hunters
to get the job done by three,
pay them a fortune.

Set your sights,
mark me as your only target.
Use two hands,
aim for my third eye—
kiss it
until you foresee our future again.

Incarcerate me
for the rest of our lives.
If I was mistaken,
I'll bear the sentence
fearlessly.
Just find me.

If it was you—
fight me.

Let me throw punches,
release the pain I hold
for how things happened.

Scream your head off at me.
Take my strikes
bravely.

It may look like I'm throwing fists—
but my hands
just want to touch you,
be near you.

Yell
as much as you need.
I'm simply glad
to hear your voice.

So take my punches
until I fall
into your arms.

And I'll take your screams
until you
whisper—
you'll never
let me go
again.

Finding Your Way Back to Yourself

There is no greater tragedy
than gifting your love
to someone unwilling to accept it.

Politely declining—
each time
you breathe your all
into those words.

So with each *I love you*,
I watched you take back
parts of you.

Chipping away
at the letters,
piece by piece,

until the words
could no longer carry
the weight of their meaning.

I love you
went to *love you*
went to *love u*
went to *luv u*
went to *luv*
went to *u.*

The Earth Speaks

You have taken
my lungs
to fill yours
with money
and things.

You cut me open
to build towers,
then asked me—
why I no longer breathe.

You paved over my skin
and wondered
why nothing soft grows.

You silenced the birds
to hear your machines better—
and now
you miss the sound of singing.

You stripped me
for comfort.
You burned me
for speed.
You drained me dry
to decorate
your emptiness.

And still—
you ask
why the storms are louder.

Why the air feels thin.
Why the seasons weep.

I gave you
everything.
And you named it
yours.

The Light at the Beginning

Leaving the world in fear
and entering it in tears,
uncertain of what this new place holds—

you were welcomed
into the arms of loving souls.

You need not fear
what the unknown holds.

For if you had been too frightened
to enter the light,
you would have never known life.

Now take that truth
and carry it with you
on your journey.

For at its end,
you cannot be worried.

SECTION IV

Reclamation and Awakening

When I started to return to myself.

Again

For me,
I will no longer give away
my skin,
my bones—
just to prove I am worthy
of being held.

I will not carve myself open
to show what I'm made of.
I already know.

For me,
I will reclaim
my energy,
my thoughts,
my time.
They are mine to give,
not mine to lose.

I will sit at the table
and savor the first bite,
and the last.

For me,
I will not cry oceans
for those who need distance.
I will swim in still waters,
close to the shore
of my own peace.

I will speak.
Even if it makes things uncomfortable.

Even if it takes us deeper
than you wanted to go.

I will lift my head.
Pick up my crown.
Let it shine,
even if yours dims.
I will not slouch
to make others seem tall.

For me,
I will stop losing
on purpose.
I will stop folding
so others can win.
I deserve the victory
of being true to myself.

For me,
I choose to be whole.
Not hollowed.
Not diminished.

For me,
I will be
enough.

The Girl I Owe

I have tears in my eyes
because I've hurt her
more times
than I can count.

I've let her down,
disappointed her,
gone against her wishes—
even when I knew better.

I've lacked the discipline
it would take
to make her proud—
to take her to new heights,
to lead her toward
the dreams she once whispered
with so much hope.

She deserves the world.
And yet,
I've limited her.
Wounded her.

I've drawn imperfections
on her body.
I've dulled her colors,
dimmed her spark.
I've closed doors
she was born to walk through.

I owe her
more than this.

And she—
I—
am still here.
Bruised, but breathing.
I press a hand
to the pulse of possibility
still beating beneath the ache.

There is time.
Time to rise,
to listen when she speaks,
to walk the paths she mapped
before I lost the way.

I will gather
every scattered piece,
every forgotten promise,
and build again—
not from shame,
but from devotion.

I will return to her
with steady hands,
with softer words,
with reverence.

And we—
we will become
the woman
she once believed
I could be.

Reframing

I have never felt
this
before.

But with you,
I feel the tremble
of something at risk—
not loss,
but the fear
that I may be too much,
or not enough,
for a love
you haven't yet named.

I am afraid.
I am afraid.
I am—
learning that fear is not a warning
but a signal:
a flicker in the dark
asking to be seen,
not followed.

So I stay still.
I loosen the old stories.
I reframe.
I reframe.

If your love asks
for a quieter version of me—

if your arms feel more
like architecture
than embrace—
then I'll trust
this is not where
my becoming belongs.

Cosmic Law

And when he comes back—
don't insult the universe
by letting him in again.

Don't undo the work
it took
to get him out of your life.

Don't dishonor
the sleepless nights,
the shattered illusions,
the aching growth
that pulled you through.

What's meant for you
stays.
It does not leave
just to test your threshold.

The world may tolerate
injustice,
but the universe
does not.

It balances.
It clears.
It protects.

And when you trust it,
it will make things right
for you
again.

Little Does She Know

How do you tell the sun
that she's the sun?

She just looks around
and sees light everywhere—
not realizing
she's the source.

She doesn't see
the shadows she chases away,
the colors she wakes,
the life she calls forward
just by rising.

She thinks warmth is everywhere—
not knowing
it radiates from her.

She thinks the world is golden—
not realizing
she's the one who gilded it.

So how do you tell the sun
that she's the sun?

You don't.
You love her in the morning,
when she rises unsure.
You stay through the clouds.
You reflect her,
so she might finally
see herself.

No Logic in Love

There is no logic in love.
No formula,
no rule,
no reason.

It arrives without warning,
leaves without permission.

There is no sense in heartbreak—
no clean edges,
no fair terms.
Only aching,
only the echo
of what once was.

There is no promise of the future.
No guarantee
that what feels eternal
will survive
the ordinary passing of time.

And now,
there is no you
in me
anymore.

Not in the way I speak.
Not in the way I dream.
Not even
in the way I break.

Unmarked

Your name—
once etched
into the deepest parts
of my brain
and body—

no longer
even rings a bell.

Oh, how grateful I am
to have moved
mountains
to get here.

The Path to Yourself

If you think you've found yourself—
if you've been allowed to believe
you know who you are—
but you've never been
completely and utterly lost,

then allow me
to set your perspective on fire.

You don't truly know
who you are
or who you want to be
until your mind holds a million thoughts
and not even one makes sense—
until you are at a complete loss
for words
and for identity.

When you've given up your beliefs,
lost sight of your goals,
and can't recognize the person in the mirror—

only then
will you find clarity in the madness.
Only then
will your own voice rise
from the tornado of voices.

The road that leads you to yourself
is bumpy, blurry, and terrifying.

But through the pain,
the confusion,
the doubt—
comes your foundation:
an unshakable,
unbreakable
sense of self-love
and understanding.

Everything will soon be clear.
At least,
I hope—
for my own sake.

When the Roles Change

Sometimes,
you must save yourself
from the people
who once saved you.

Because time moves.
Hearts harden. Pain changes people—
and sometimes,
they don't notice.

What was once a lifeline
can become a leash.
What once held you up
can start to hold you back.

And the hardest part
is not the leaving.
It's the knowing—
that love doesn't always grow
with you.

That safety
can turn into silence.
That comfort
can become a cage.

So you walk away.
Not with anger.
Not with blame.
But with the quiet
truth that, this time,
you must choose *you*.

Fault Line

Right when the dust has settled on your skin,
and you rise—shaky, but finally upright,
right when your breath no longer tastes like ash,
and the mirror reflects more than just survival,

just when your spine remembers it's strong,
and your voice no longer flinches at silence,
right when your hands build something steady—
walls that don't shake at every tremor of doubt,

just when you dare to whisper, *maybe this is peace,*
and the storm seems to have forgotten your
name—
that's when it begins again:
the shattering, the unmaking, the fall.

The ground you trusted splits like a secret.
The sky you prayed under folds in on itself.
And you are left—rubble again—
wondering why hope is always the first to bleed.

But still, beneath the ruin, you breathe.
Still, you gather what remains,
because if you've learned anything—
it's how to build,
even when it breaks.

Who You've Always Been

He didn't want you to know
you could swim on your own,
so he pretended to be your life jacket.

He didn't want you to know
you could breathe on your own,
so he told you he was your oxygen.

He didn't want you to fly,
so he led you to believe
you didn't have wings.

He left you feeling helpless.

But darling—
oh, darling—

you have a dolphin's tail.
The very air aches
for the privilege of filling your lungs.

All the eagles wait,
watching in awe,
for the moment you take flight.

So swim.
Breathe.
Fly.

You have always been
everything you need.

The One Who Got Away

I guess I was
"the one who got away."

And I wonder—
about all the poets
and artists
who write and sing
about me.

Do they live in daydreams,
in the thoughts
of what could've been?
Or do they wither
under the weight of "what ifs"?

How often do I run
across their minds each day?
And do they remember me
accurately—
for who I truly was,
and not
for the person
they wanted me to become?

Not the role
they hoped I'd play,
the void
they thought I'd fill.

Because I don't believe
in the ones who got away.

I believe
they serve as lifelong lessons—
constant reminders
to seize moments,
to be bold,
to be vulnerable,
to leave no love unexpressed,
no feeling unspoken.

I believe in time and space—
how they marvelously
come together.
I believe
they make no mistakes.

So to all the poets
and artists—
think of me
the next time
you choose courage.

Allow me
to dance across your mind
when she's standing there,
before you—
and you're brave enough
to tell her
that you love her,
too.

Confinement

A fortress—
with walls so high
I've lost sight
of the world beyond them.

I built it
stone by stone,
each one shaped by fear,
by memory,
by the ache of being
too open,
too soon.

Now I wander
the quiet halls of my own making,
searching for the door
I once sealed shut.

And I'll keep searching—
quietly,
bravely,
blindly—
until love finds its way in.
Or I find the courage
to let it.

Softness Up Close

From afar,
she looked somber—
a dark silhouette,
as if she were lost
in a world
of her own making.

But when you stepped closer,
and reached out a hand
to touch her,
she unfolded.

She embodied a softness
so complete,
so sure,
it wrapped around you
like warm silk.

She offered a place
for weary heads to settle,
a quiet ease
for the restless.

And even after you left,
the memory of her touch—
the residue of her skin—
lingered on your hands,
a reminder
that peace exists.

When others pulled at her stems,
tore her petals,
left her bruised and broken,
she grew back softer still.

Because she knew:
the unkind
need kindness the most.

They wanted her sharp,
armored, unfeeling.
But she stayed tender—
and that was her rebellion.

The Sun Is My Lover

Today, when they ask me how I'm doing,
I say,
"well."

Tomorrow,
I hope I can mean it.

As I sit in the sun,
I allow its warmth
to thaw the parts of me
that have hardened over time.

Its rays
pierce through the armor
I built to shield myself
from life's sharpest weapons.

Today,
I surrender that armor.

I allow myself to soften—
to let the light
reach the corners
I've always kept hidden,
protected.

I let the world in.

Wholeheartedly
surrendering,
I expose myself
to the sun—

to its kind warmth,
to the risk
of getting burned.

I choose
its beautiful and bright rays,
even if they pose
a danger to me.

I'll take my chances
on being hurt
over the fear
of shying away.

And I so choose
to do the same
with you.

The Universe Inside Me

I guess I'm frustrated.
I guess I'm confused.
How do you not see
that I carry the entire universe
inside of me?

How can you miss the warmth
radiating from my chest—
thawing the world as it turns,
cradling the cold
into comfort?

The source that lights our skies
burns in my soul,
and I've let it shine
so you wouldn't have to stumble in the dark.

Those mountains you love?
They rose because the earth
folded and arched itself
under my footsteps,
to lift me
closer
to the stars I placed
so carefully in the sky.

And the ocean—
oh, the ocean.
That's where I keep my secrets,
the ones too sacred to name.

So yes,
I'm frustrated.
Because if you really saw me—
you'd know the whole world
was already in my hands.

Where Love Goes

When you left,
I had all this love to give—
nowhere to place it,
no hands to hold it.

So I gave it anyway.

To the stranger I passed on the street,
to the tired cashier,
to the sidewalk,
to the sky.

And slowly,
my surroundings
started to shimmer.

The world
grew warmer,
brighter.

Because love,
when not hoarded,
returns.

It echoed off faces
and windows
and trees—
and in the light.

I saw you less,
but I felt myself
more.

The Free Ones

I think the people
who can love who they want
are the freest souls in the world.
The rest of us, are just pretending—
holding hands in shadows,
building cages out of duty,
and naming them "choices."

We smile like actors
in roles we didn't write,
applauding the stories
we dare not live.

In the name of what?
Honor?
Fear?

What weight do we carry
that love cannot lift?

The free ones—they move like wind,
unapologetic and unhidden,
not asking permission
to feel
to reach
to be.

And we, the tethered,
watch them—
jealous,
righteous,
lonely.

Not Everything Green Will Grow

Why are you planting a flower
that refuses
to take to your soil?

Why are you pouring yourself
into something
that wilts
no matter how gently
you water it?

You soften your hands,
adjust the light,
change the timing—
and still,
it does not bloom for you.

The soil isn't the problem.
Your roots are deep,
your ground is rich.
You are capable
of growing forests.

But some seeds
were never meant
to bloom in your garden.

They Hold No Fire

You can't borrow something
from someone
who doesn't own it.

You can't ask for love
from someone
who's never known it.

You can pour yourself out
waiting for a return
that will never come—
not because they're cruel,
but because they're empty.

You can beg them
to hold you gently,
but they don't know
what gentle feels like.

You can write poems
about a kind of love
they've never seen—
and wonder why
they never answer them.

Some people
aren't withholding.
They've just never held a flame—
never known warmth
enough to give it.

SECTION V

Love and Becoming

Who I became, despite it all.

The Ride of a Lifetime

I'm not supposed to know
who built the rollercoaster—
what tools they used,
what blueprints they followed,
or what logic shaped the loops.

It's not my job
to understand the route—
if it goes forward,
backward,
spins me sideways
or leaves me hanging upside down
in midair.

I don't need to know
how high the drop is,
or when it's coming.
I don't want to.

I'm just here
for the ride.

And yes—
I'm scared.
My stomach's in knots,
my heart is pounding,
and I've braced for impact
more times than I can count.

But even fear
is part of the thrill.

Even the unknown
holds something holy.

And somewhere deep down,
I trust
that when the ride slows,
when the track straightens out,
and the lights come on,

I'll be glad
I buckled in,
held on,
and let it take me.

The Quiet Rescue

You were saving me
when you gave love
without asking.

You were saving me
when you offered time
without counting.

You were saving me
when you made me laugh
without trying.

You were saving me
when you remained patient
as I stumbled through healing.

You never asked me
to be anything
other than who I was
in that moment.

With love that asked for nothing in return.
With feelings that never shifted with the wind.
With a presence so steady
it gave me permission
to be soft again.

You didn't come to rescue me—
but you did.
In the quietest
and truest ways.

Where Your Breath Lives

I love the way
your arms wrap around me
as we lay here,
side by side.

Your heartbeat in my ear—
a steady tide of comfort.
Your breath, slow and deep,
a lullaby I never want to end.

I listen for it—
that exhale,
that quiet sigh of peace.

A sound so distinct
it tells me
you're here,
really here.

Holding me,
breathing me in,
as if time itself
were something sacred
between your lungs.

So let us stay like this—
no rush,
no words,
just breath and skin
and silence shared.

For in your breathing,
in that sigh,
the world softens—
and so do I.

Between each breath
you take beside me,
I'm reminded:
that's where I feel alive, too.

Ode to My Lover's Back

I have memorized the map of your back—
each curve, each scar, each quiet story
etched in muscle and skin.
It is the place I press my forehead
when words grow too small
for the size of my love.

Your back carries the weight
of silent burdens,
yet never once turns away.
It is the shield I reach for
when the world feels sharp,
the anchor that holds
when I drift too far.

I watch it rise with breath,
a quiet rhythm
steady as truth,
and I wonder how something
can be both fortress
and field.

Your back—
broad as dusk,
tender as dawn—
is the compass
I follow without fear.

Topography

I can map out the lines on your face
like constellations,
reading the creases near your eyes
like rivers etched by time.

Your skin is a geography I know by heart—
the freckle beneath your jaw,
the slope of your cheekbone,
the way your smile breaks like morning
over uncertain ground.

I trace the curve of your brow
as if it were a path
leading me through years
I wish I could relive again and again.

I can map the journey
by memory alone—
turn left at your laugh,
rest at the hollow of your collar,
follow the warmth between your shoulder blades
until I reach
the quiet room
where I am known.

You are
the map,
the trail,
and the destination.

And every time
I lose myself,
I trace the lines on your face—
until I find
my way
back home.

Two Weeks

I want to jump on the next train,
board the first plane out,
chase the quickest route
into your arms.

But I'll be patient.
I've done it for twenty-five years—
what's another two weeks?

Still, I want to run to you,
be close enough
to touch your smile
when I make you laugh.

I don't want to talk.
I just want to be—
by you,
breathe beside you,
exist where your presence softens the air.

They say,
Why rush?
If they're your person, you'll have forever.
There's no need to hurry now.

But those people
have never met you.
And those people
have never felt your presence
to know
how suffocating it is
to be without it.

Seasons of You

From now on,
I only want to swim in oceans
where the algae sway—
mirroring the green hue
of your eyes.

I only want to wander
through forests
where autumn's leaves
change with grace,
echoing the quiet strength
of your soul.

From now on,
my rest will be your chest—
the place I lay my head
and let the world dissolve,
lulled to sleep
by the rhythm
of your heartbeat.

Your back
is the only shield I need,
the only home
I wish to guard.

You are
the first breath of air
I've drawn in ages—
lungs full,
heart quiet,
worry free.

Exhibit

We have a love
that others admire.
They watch us—
gazing in awe,
as if we were something rare.

They frame the way
we look at each other and smile,
sketch portraits
of my head resting
softly on your shoulder.

Ours is the kind of love
that breaks the lens
of a photographer's camera—
too vivid
to be captured,
too alive
to be still.

They try to bottle our spark,
place it in a glass box,
display it in museums
under soft lights,
as if our love were art
that needed explaining.

They chase the glow
we leave behind—
never realizing
the fire lives
only between us.

Sometimes

Some time has passed.
And
sometimes,
I wish I had never met you.

Like when the only place
I can fall soundly asleep
is in your bed.
Or when the only place
I want to rest my head
is on your chest.

Sometimes,
I wish I had never met you.
Like when I remember your lips—
soft,
like your words.
Your kiss—
gentle, like your touch.

Or when I think of your heart—
patient,
like your mind.
Your thoughts—
vast
and kind.

Sometimes,
I wish I had never met you.

But
sometimes,
it feels better to know
that a fire can burn
inside the calmest soul.

It feels better to know
that a love like yours exists.

Stable. Steady.
A slow burn,
that warmed me
for some time.

When the Wicks Align

We are like two wicks
in the same candle.

When we burn together—
in rhythm,
in sync—
we generate more than light.
We create warmth.
Enough to reach
everyone around us.

But when we burn out of time,
when one flickers
and the other fights for flame,
the heat fades.
The glow dims.

We were meant
to rise together.
To steady each other's fire
when the wax runs low.

So when the wind comes—
as it always does—
let us lean inward,
shield each other's flame.

Let us remember:
our light is brightest
not when we burn alone,
but when we burn as one.

Bahar *(Spring)*

Head in the skies,
heart in the trees,
soul in the stars,
and hope in the leaves—
I am everywhere but here.

My thoughts consist of clouds and dreams.
My heart feels for everything the wind touches.
My soul houses galaxies,
and my hope sways with the leaves.

See, recently the sun has been coming out,
and lately I've been basking in its healing warmth.

The birds at dawn chirp for me to awaken.
The trees are smiling—
finally getting their beloved sun back.

I've missed this gentle wind on my face,
and the smell of spring:
a mix of fresh breeze
and the sunscreen on my skin.

I feel comfortable once again.
I feel at home.

What You Focus on Grows

I planted seeds
without knowing.
Watered the weeds
with my attention.

I stared at what I didn't want—
the fake smiles,
the insecure laughter,
the shadows dressed as people
who only saw darkness in others.

I wondered why
my garden looked like a storm.

But then—
I changed the lens.
I stopped feeding
what drained me.
Started seeking
what fed me.

I pictured the friends
I actually wanted.
Secure, open,
gentle with truth,
loud with love,
eyes wide enough
to see more than themselves.

And that's who arrived.
Or maybe—
that's who I finally saw.

Because what you focus on
grows.

So now I plant
with intention.
I guard my gaze
like sacred soil.

And the garden?
It blooms with joy
I once thought impossible.

Sanctuary

Friendship is a place of solace—
a warm soul to thaw in
when the outside world leaves you cold.

A heart that holds you
when your home falls apart.
A mind that steadies you
when you're out of breath.

Eyes that see you
when you've lost your sight.

Friendship is a place of solace.
And I've carved out
a little space for myself.

I think
I'm going to stay
a while.

Boxing Classes

They ask me where I stand—
as if I must plant flags
on every hill they've mapped and manned.
But I move like water—
not to escape,
but because truth is rarely still.

They want lines.
Edges.
Declarations carved in stone.
They want to say *you said*,
trap me in tone,
mark and store me,
like a barcode on bone.

They need their "friends"
arranged in aisles,
neatly shelved,
monitored—
in a misguided attempt
to locate their own identity.

But I won't play that game.

I don't fit in their cardboard certainty.
Their need to define me
says more about their fear
than my freedom.
They want me tame, predictable,
so they can measure their worth
against mine again.

They're shaky, brittle, unsteady—
not because I'm unclear,
but because every time
I break the box they built for me,
their narrow reality
bends with it.

There is more to the world
than walls and corners.
There are questions
meant to be lived,
not answered.
There are people
meant to be experienced,
not categorized.

I pray they pause—
just long enough to see
the box they crafted
was their own cage, not me.
And I pray it breaks,
so they finally breathe
and remember the air
that exists beyond their grief.

What Can't Be Bought

I can't afford your entrance fee—
you charge in pride, in power,
in cold shoulders
and louder voices.
But I live my life
in a different currency.

I pay in softness,
in truth that trembles,
in the quiet offering
of my open palms.
I spend my time
building safety,
not walls.

You want gold-plated love,
polished and performative,
but mine is made of river stones—
weathered, honest,
meant to be held,
not displayed.

I could never match your cost.
And I no longer try.
Because I've learned
the richest hearts
don't need
to buy their way inside.

Maybe

Maybe it's how he hugs me
with his eyes.
Or how his smile
warms my entire body.

Maybe it's that his soul
whispers to mine,
pulling us closer.

Maybe it's meant to be.

Or maybe—
it'll just be me.

Alchemy of Me

I am destined for greatness—
in my own way,
by my own definition of the word.

I am a carefully crafted concoction—
a spell cast with intention.

Empathy,
compassion,
kindness.

Introspection—
quiet as moonlight.
The pulse of nature.
The fire of art.
Music. Poetry.
The things that make me feel.

And a whole lot of magic—
the kind tucked into corners of the world,
in whispers of the ancient,
echoes of the seven wonders,
stitched through me
like constellations on skin.

Skin and soul.
Root and reach.
A touch that grounds.
A thought that lifts.

This is my spell.
This is my greatness.

Be Productive

"Be productive."
The sound hits my ears every time,
but never lands right.

What am I producing?
Does *produce* mean *value*?

No, that can't be right—
the produce section of the grocery store
isn't always the most expensive.

Does *production* mean *worth*?
Are we calculating production value
like our life is a film?

"Productive."
The sound always grazes my ears,
but never settles right.

To be productive
means to be someone I'm not—
a cog in your machine.

But I don't work in your factory.
And I don't live in your world.

Find me outside,
running in the grass,
holding hands with squirrels,
feeding nuts to the children.

Create—
that is what I do.

I create beauty in the gloom,
love in the strange,
connection in the separation,
and life
in the stillness.

Dare I resist productivity
in the world of medicine—
a never-ending conveyor belt
producing depleted shells of people
who no longer know how to convey…
well, anything?

How do they give
what they no longer have?
How do they provide
what was never provided to them?

"Productive."
I do not aspire to be productive.

I aspire to be *human.*

"Be human."
That is the greatest feat of all.

Quantum Creator

Today,
you carve the life
you will live tomorrow.

You hold the tools—
steady in your hands,
sharp with possibility.
What will you shape?

Today,
you paint the canvas
that will step out of its frame
and become your world.

You have all the colors.
You have the brush.
What will you create?

Every word,
every thought,
every action—
they chisel,
they shade,
they stitch the future
into being.

So pause.
Look at your hands.
They're full of power.

What will you choose
to bring to life?

No Time

"There is no time," they say.
And I smile.
Because I know what that means.

It means I'm busy—
but not the kind that drains,
the kind that drives.

I'm occupied,
enthralled,
entirely consumed
by the work that stirs my soul.

So immersed in doing what I love
that I forget to eat—
not out of neglect,
but because hunger
has taken a new shape.

I am fed
by the fire of purpose,
the steady burn of passion,
the quiet rhythm of becoming
everything I'm meant to be.

There is no time—
and what a beautiful thing
that is.

Where Silence Speaks

All may listen—
but few truly *hear*.
Not just the words,
but the weight behind them.
Not just the sound,
but the silence that follows.

All may watch—
but few truly *see*.
Not just the face,
but the flicker in the eyes.
Not just the body,
but the shift in the shoulders,
the story in the stillness.

It's easy to observe.
Harder to understand.

And rarer still
to stay.

So when you find someone
who hears you
in the hush between your words—
who sees you
in the moments you fade—
hold them like breath,
like light you thought was lost.
Because they are few,
and they do not come twice.

I Am Like the Sunset

I am vast and ever-changing,
yet consistent and reliable.
I am composed of many hues,
though my light wavers.
I am bold and demanding,
yet subtle and discreet.

I cannot be replicated;
you will never find the same version of me twice.
I am purposefully crafted—
beyond what language can contain.

I cannot be captured or shown
to those who haven't made the quest—
to pursue me with intention,
and spend their presence with me.

No technology can capture my true essence.
I demand all five senses.
I require patience and intellect,
purpose and confidence.

I do not care to be understood by the masses.
I do not care for them to see me, to know me.
For if they do not have the courage to quest,
they lack the mind I find worthy.

So when I say I'm seeking someone who sees me,
I mean I want someone who understands
the force of nature before them—
a power most people take for granted
day after day.

I may share my warmth and beauty with all,
but I share my love and power
with those who love me—
not in passing—
but because they have come to unerringly
see
and *know me.*

The Universe Is Listening

The universe whispers
in the breath between thoughts.
It leaves gifts in quiet places,
in hands we almost didn't reach for,
in moments we nearly overlooked.

It knows what we long for.
It listens to our focus,
our fire,
our most fragile hope.

What we seek,
we begin to shape.
What we believe,
we begin to hold.

So tend to your attention.
Let it bloom in love.
Let it rest in peace.
Let it shine in joy.

And watch—
watch the world respond.

For the universe always gives—
not when we demand,
but when we align.

For the One Who's Waiting

The things that let me feel
the most deeply
are the very things
that help me write
the most beautifully.

So take it—
have it world.

The ache,
the softness,
the unbearable swell of feeling.

Because somewhere,
someone is waiting.

Patiently.
Quietly.
For these words
to kiss paper

and give them
what they haven't found
anywhere else—

the feeling
of home.

Author's Note

These poems were born in moments when I had
no choice but to write—when silence grew too
heavy, and what I felt demanded release.

I write for my family—for those who came before
me—whose inheritance was the gold hidden in
the flame.

This is not just a book of poems. It is my heart.
My voice. My blood memory. My quiet rebellion.

This is how I survived.
This is my story—
in ink, and in blood.
And how, together, I turned them into something
golden.

About the Author

Dana Hazem is a poet, writer, and medical student whose work explores healing, identity, love, and the emotional landscapes we're often taught to silence. Born in Germany to Afghan parents and raised in the Bay Area of California, Dana grew up surrounded by a deep cultural legacy of music, poetry, history, and art. Those roots shaped her— grounding her in storytelling and creative expression from an early age.

In poetry, she found a safe place to process pain, release emotion, and stay grounded. It became her escape, her companion, and ultimately, her form of transformation. While her academic passion led her to medicine, Dana continues to write as a way of understanding herself and the world around her.

Alchemy of Ink and Blood is her debut poetry collection.

Follow along at
@quietrebellionpress